Walter Foster
Jr.

learn to draw
Safari
Animals

Step-by-step instructions
for 25 exotic animals

ILLUSTRATED BY ROBBIN CUDDY

Quarto is the authority on a wide range of topics.
Quarto educates, entertains, and enriches the lives of our readers—
enthusiasts and lovers of hands-on living.
www.quartoknows.com

6 Orchard Road, Suite 100
Lake Forest, CA 92630
quartoknows.com
Visit our blogs @quartoknows.com

MIX
Paper from
responsible sources
FSC® C101537

Printed in China
1 3 5 7 9 10 8 6 4 2

Table of Contents

Tools & Materials

There's more than one way to bring safari animals to life on paper—you can use crayons, markers, colored pencils, or even paints. Just be sure you have plenty of good animal colors—yellows, reds, grays, and browns.

drawing pencil
and paper

eraser

sharpener

colored
pencils

felt-tip markers

paintbrushes
and paints

How to Use This Book

The drawings in this book are made up of basic shapes, such as circles, triangles, and rectangles. Practice drawing the shapes below.

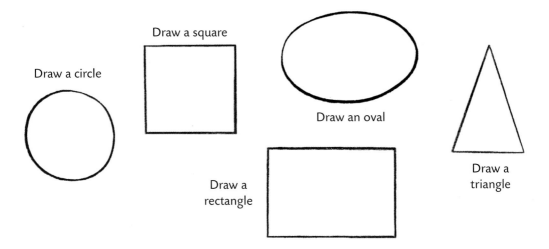

Draw a circle

Draw a square

Draw an oval

Draw a rectangle

Draw a triangle

Notice how these drawings begin with basic shapes.

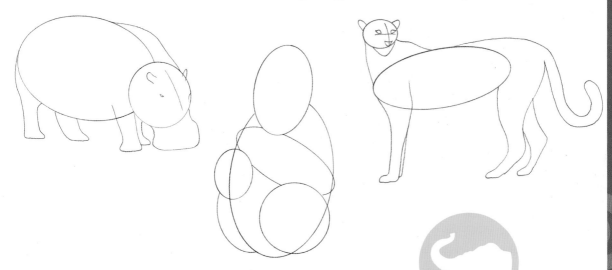

In this book, you'll learn different facts about each featured safari animal. Look for mini quizzes along the way to see what you know!

Look for this symbol, and check your answers on page 40!

African Elephant

Location:
African savannas, grasslands, and forests

Size: 14 feet tall at the shoulder
Weight: 8 tons

Did You Know?

An African elephant's trunk has two "fingers" at the tip for grabbing and foraging. The trunk is also used for drinking, breathing, and even hugging other elephants.

Diet: Grasses, bushes, fruit, and other plants

African elephants are the largest land mammals alive today. These intelligent creatures have wide ears, long trunks, ivory tusks, and thick, wrinkly skin.

Fun Fact!

Just like dolphins, humans, and the great apes, elephants have the ability to recognize themselves in mirrors!

Gazelle

Gazelles are known for their unique bounding run. These fast, graceful animals have hoofed feet, ringed horns, and bodies similar to deer.

Mini Quiz

True or false:
Gazelles are solitary animals and prefer to travel alone.

(Answer on page 40)

Giraffe

The giraffe has a very long neck, tall legs, a pair of horns, and a wiry tail.
The tallest land animal on earth, a male giraffe can reach 19 feet tall!

Giraffes are surprisingly fast; they can run more than 30 miles per hour!

Fun Fact!

Lion

Details

Size: Up to 40 inches tall
Weight: Up to 500 pounds
Diet: Antelopes, zebras, wildebeests, monkeys, hippos, and more
Location: African grasslands and savannas, India's Gir Forest

Did You Know?

Adult male and female lions look quite a bit different from each other. A male lion has a large mane around its head and neck and is much larger, sometimes weighing hundreds of pounds more than a female.

Dubbed "King of Beasts," the lion is a large, regal feline that lives in a *pride* (or group). Lions use their deep, distinct roar to define their pride's territory.

Fun Fact!

Born blind, lions do not open their eyes until one to two weeks after birth. They are also born with spots on their coats, which fade as the lions mature.

Lemur

Details

Size: 3.5 to 28 inches long, not including the tail
Weight: Up to 15 pounds
Diet: Leaves, fruits, insects, and birds' eggs
Location: Madagascar and the Comoros Islands

Did You Know?

A lemur's eyes work well in low light, giving them great night vision.

Lemurs are monkey-like primates that have round eyes, small muzzles, and five fingers on each hand and foot. They spend most of their time among the trees.

1

2

3

4

5

6

7

Mini Quiz

Which of the following is the smallest species of lemur?
A. Ring-tailed lemur
B. Madame Berthe's mouse lemur
C. Black lemur
D. Brown mouse lemur
(Answer on page 40)

Impala

An impala is a slender antelope with a long neck, a pair of wavy horns, and a two-toned coat with white markings.

Fun Fact!

The world's fiercest predators, including lions and cheetahs, hunt the impala. Fortunately impalas are swift runners that can leap as far as 33 feet!

Kangaroo

The kangaroo has large ears, a small mouth, and powerful hind legs. Its long, tapering tail helps the kangaroo balance while standing still.

Mini Quiz

How high can a kangaroo jump?
A. 2 feet
B. 3 feet
C. 6 feet
D. 10 feet

(Answer on page 40)

Leopard

Size: Nearly 30 inches tall at the shoulder
Weight: 200 pounds

Diet: Meat from deer, antelope, and other prey

Location: Africa and Asia

Did You Know?

Leopards often bring their food up into the trees to protect it from other animals.

Known for its beautifully spotted coat, this striking feline is skilled at hunting, running, swimming, and climbing trees.

Fun Fact!

How can you tell a leopard from a jaguar? Look at the coat! A jaguar's markings (called "rosettes") contain black spots.

Meerkat

Meerkats are adorable critters with pointed muzzles and black eye patches. They are social animals that live in packs of about 5 to 25 individuals.

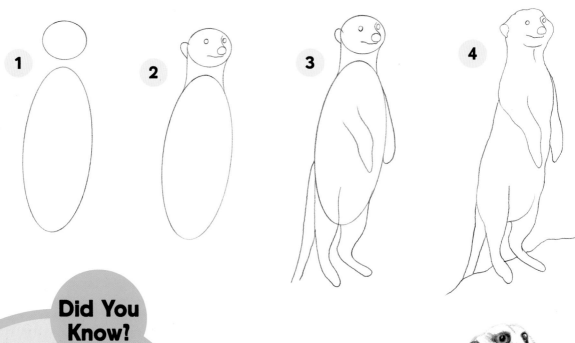

1   2   3   4

Did You Know?

Meerkats live in complex burrows made up of underground tunnels and chambers. These homes stay cool even on the hottest days.

5

6

Okapi

This hoofed animal is known for its very distinct coloring. It has a reddish-brown body, black-and-white striped legs, and white facial markings.

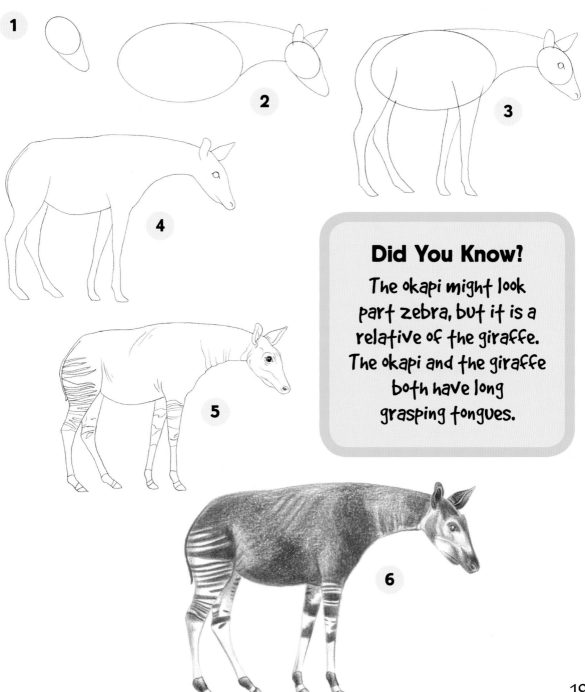

Did You Know?

The okapi might look part zebra, but it is a relative of the giraffe. The okapi and the giraffe both have long grasping tongues.

Hippopotamus

These large creatures have little round ears, bulging eyes, and thick gray skin. They can open their mouths very wide to show off their giant teeth.

1

2

Fun Fact!

Hippopotamus means "river horse" in Greek. These graceful swimmers can actually walk on the bottoms of lakes and rivers.

3

4

5

6

Hyena

The hyena is a mischievous carnivore that resembles a wild dog. A skilled hunter and scavenger, this animal has a powerful jaw, neck, and shoulders for tearing apart prey.

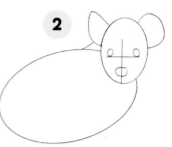

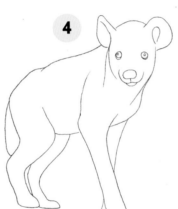

Mini Quiz

What is the term for a group of hyenas that live together?
A. Pack
B. Pod
C. Herd
D. Cackle
(Answer on page 40)

Mountain Gorilla

Size: Up to 6 feet tall (while standing)
Weight: Up to 485 pounds

Diet: Leaves, shoots, roots, and fruit

Fun Fact!

Mountain gorillas are extremely intelligent animals and can learn sign language!

Location: African tropical forests

Mountain gorillas are among the world's largest primates. They have hairless faces, large nostrils, and a distinct brow ridge.

1

2

Mini Quiz

True or false:
Mountain gorillas
generally walk
upright on their
hind legs like
humans.

(Answer on page 40)

3

4

5

6

23

Oryx

The oryx is an antelope with a full chest, long legs, and two thin, lengthy horns. Their coats range in color from white and gray to brown and red.

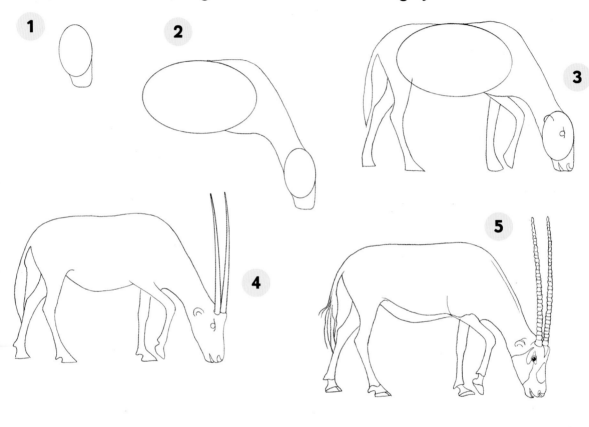

Did You Know!

The oryx is well adapted to the desert heat. This animal has a special nose with lots of capillaries that cool its blood as it breathes.

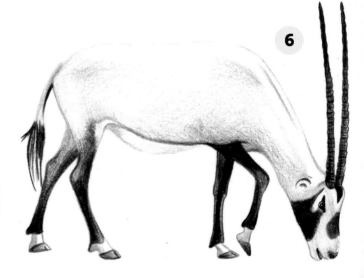

Bat-Eared Fox

The bat-eared fox has large, wide ears and a small, pointed face. This canine has a yellow and gray grizzled coat with darker fur on its face, legs, and tail.

Fun Fact!

The bat-eared fox loves to eat termites. one fox can eat more than a million termites per year!

Nile Crocodile

Details

Size: Up to 20 feet long
Weight: 500 to 2,000 pounds
Diet: Fish, birds, and a variety of other animals
Location: Madagascar, the Nile Basin, and sub-Saharan Africa

Did You Know?

Crocodiles spend most of their time in water, such as rivers, estuaries, and marshlands. As they swim, they keep most of their body hidden while their nostrils, ears, and eyes poke above the surface.

One of the largest reptiles on earth, the Nile crocodile is a stealthy predator with thick, plated skin and a long snout full of sharp teeth.

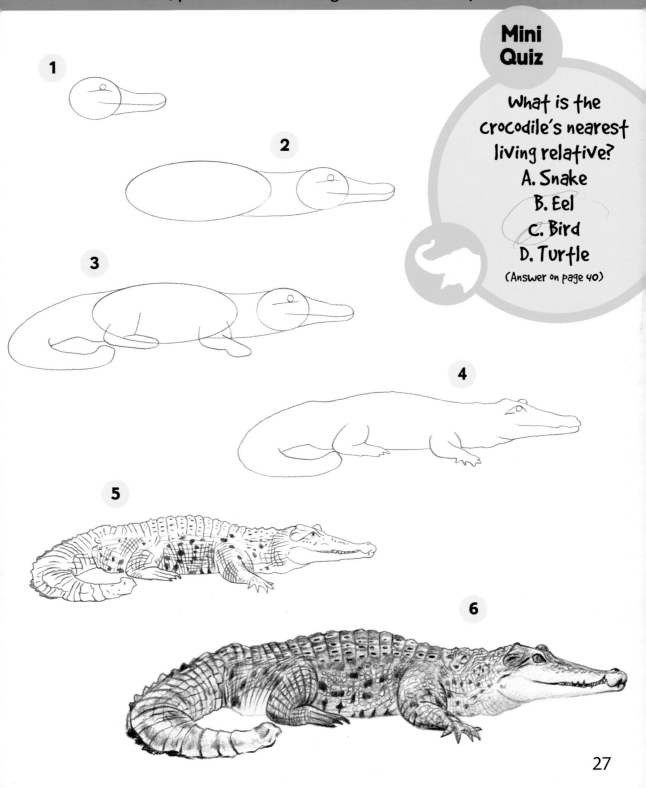

1

2

3

4

5

6

27

Baboon

The baboon is an aggressive monkey with a long snout and a long, arched tail. These social animals communicate through vocalizations, gestures, and expressions.

Fun Fact!

Baboons are born with black hair and pink faces, ears, and hands. over time, their hair changes color and their skin turns brown.

28

Aardvark

The aardvark has small eyes, large ears, a thick tail, and spade-like claws. It uses its long, sensitive snout to find food in the ground.

Mini Quiz

What does the word "aardvark" mean in the Afrikaans language?
A. Short kangaroo
B. Insect eater
C. Tongue digger
D. Earth pig
(Answer on page 40)

Cheetah

Details

Size: Up to 3 feet tall
Weight: 75 to 140 pounds
Diet: Birds, rabbits, and antelopes
Location: Grasslands of Africa

Fun Fact!

The cheetah is earth's fastest land animal, reaching speeds of more than 70 miles per hour!

This furry feline has a black-spotted yellow coat with a white underbelly. Its long legs, spine, and powerful paws make it an incredibly fast predator.

Mini Quiz

True or false: Cheetahs can go more than four days without a drink of water.

(Answer on page 40)

1

2

3

4

5

6

31

Wildebeest

Also called a "gnu," the wildebeest is a large, ox-like antelope. It has a long tail, beard, and mane and a set of thick, sharp horns that curl forward.

1

2

3

Fun Fact!

The wildebeest migration in late May is a spectacular event. More than 1.5 million wildebeests travel north through the Serengeti in search of water and food.

4

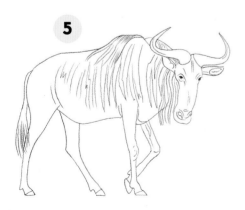

5

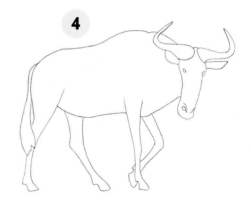

6

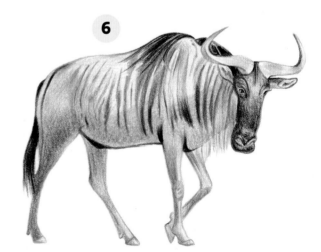

Yellow Mongoose

The yellow mongoose is a small mammal with a long body and white-tipped tail. Their grizzled coats range from gray to yellow and orange.

Fun Fact!

Yellow mongooses live in colonies that inhabit underground burrow systems. Sometimes they share burrows and tunnels with squirrels and meerkats.

Zebra

Size: Up to 5 feet tall at the shoulder
Weight: 450 to 1,000 pounds

Diet: Grasses

Location: African grasslands

Did You Know?

Zebras can sleep standing up! To protect themselves, zebras sleep only when huddled together in a large group.